Cont

Introduction

I was very popular when I became president of the United States in 1961. At forty-three years old, I was the youngest president ever elected. I was admired by many, thanks to my finely tailored suits, beautiful and stylish wife, Jackie, and my adorable young children, Caroline and John. I was an **idealistic** man with everything ahead of me—and Americans of all backgrounds were ready to share in the excitement of my youthful idealism.

I wanted to do a lot with the energy I brought to the White House, and the public was just as enthusiastic. It was a time of change, and, as I said in my inaugural address, it was a chance to fight "the common enemies of man: **tyranny**, poverty, disease, and war itself." That speech really inspired people and has gone down as one

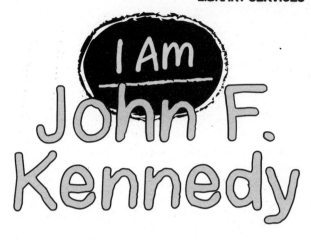

I Am John F. Kennedy

By Grace Norwich

Illustrated by
Anthony VanArsdale

SCHOLASTIC INC.

No part of this publication may be reproduced, stored in a retrieval system, or transmitted in any form or by any means, electronic, mechanical, photocopying, recording, or otherwise, without written permission of the publisher. For information regarding permission, write to Scholastic Inc., Attention: Permissions Department, 557 Broadway, New York, NY 10012.

Copyright © 2013 by Scholastic Inc.

All rights reserved. Published by Scholastic Inc.
SCHOLASTIC and associated logos are trademarks and/or registered trademarks of Scholastic Inc.

ISBN 978-0-545-56883-8

10 9 8 7 6 5 4 3   14 15 16 17 18/0

Printed in the U.S.A.   40
First printing, September 2013

Cover illustration by Mark Fredrickson
Interior illustrations by Anthony VanArsdale

of the best in modern history. In fact, one line in particular is very famous: "And so, my fellow Americans, ask not what your country can do for you; ask what you can do for your country."

It's hard to imagine that someone like me—handsome, wealthy, powerful, *and* a good speaker—hadn't always been on top of the world. But it's true. Growing up, I was a very sickly child, and I had to stay home from school a lot. I was second best to my older brother, Joe, in everything from school to sports. He was my dad's favorite and the one my father hoped would become president of the United States one day.

I never gave up, though. I used my time at home from school to become a big reader. I also loved writing and became the only president to win a Pulitzer Prize for a book I wrote. I became a hero during World War II by saving

men from our sinking ship, despite the fact that my health problems left me weak all my life. And, of course, *I* was the one to become president. I am John F. Kennedy.

People You Will Meet

JOHN "JACK" FITZGERALD KENNEDY: The thirty—fifth president of the United States was the youngest man ever elected to the position.

JOSEPH KENNEDY, SR.: Jack's dad, a wealthy and powerful man who expected all of his children to excel. He pushed Jack into politics.

ROSE KENNEDY: Jack's mom. She came from a powerful Boston Irish family and was a distant mother, though she put all her energy behind her son's political efforts.

JOSEPH KENNEDY, JR.: The eldest of the nine Kennedy children, he had a fierce rivalry with his younger brother Jack.

ROBERT "BOBBY" KENNEDY:
Jack's second–youngest
brother. He managed his
brother's presidential campaign
and gave Jack great advice.

**JACQUELINE LEE
BOUVIER KENNEDY:**
Jack's wife and mother of his two
children, Caroline and John. She
was admired for her legendary
style and grace.

LYNDON BAINES JOHNSON:
The Senate majority leader. He
became Jack's unlikely vice
president after losing the Democratic
nomination to him.

RICHARD NIXON:
The Republican vice president and
much more experienced politician who
ran against Jack for president and
lost. He was later elected president.

NIKITA KHRUSHCHEV:
The leader of the Soviet Union,
which was an enemy of the United
States during Jack's presidency.

MARTIN LUTHER KING, JR.:
The leader of the civil–rights
movement found a big
supporter in Jack.

Time Line

May 29, 1917

John "Jack" Fitzgerald Kennedy is born in Brookline, Massachusetts.

1936

Jack transfers to Harvard University after a brief time at Princeton.

1946

Jack is elected to the U.S. House of Representatives from Massachusetts and begins his political career.

1947

Jack is diagnosed with Addison's disease.

1952

Jack is elected to the U.S. Senate.

1957

Profiles in Courage, Jack's book about valiant U.S. senators, wins a Pulitzer Prize.

November 27, 1957

Jack's first child, Caroline, is born.

November 8, 1960

Jack is the youngest person to be elected president of the United States.

October 16, 1962

The United States learns the Soviet Union is building nuclear missiles in Cuba, which begins the thirteen-day confrontation between the two countries, known as the Cuban Missile Crisis.

August 5, 1963

The United States, the Soviet Union, and the United Kingdom sign the Limited Nuclear Test Ban Treaty after eight years of tough negotiations.

August 2, 1943

As commander of a torpedo boat during World War II, Jack saves many of his crew members after a Japanese destroyer sinks their boat. He is later awarded the Purple Heart for his heroic actions.

August 12, 1944

Jack's eldest brother, Joe Jr., dies when his air force plane explodes.

September 12, 1953

Jack and Jacqueline Bouvier marry in Newport, Rhode Island.

1954–1955

Jack undergoes two dangerous back operations.

November 25, 1960

Jack's son, John F. Kennedy, Jr., is born.

1961

Jack creates the Peace Corps, a government–run volunteer program that sends Americans to work abroad.

April 17, 1961

Jack authorizes the Bay of Pigs invasion in Cuba, which is defeated by Fidel Castro within three days.

November 22, 1963

Jack is assassinated in Dallas, Texas.

November 25, 1963

Jack is buried in Arlington National Cemetery in Arlington, Virginia.

12

CHAPTER
ONE

In His Brother's Shadow

When John Fitzgerald Kennedy was born on May 29, 1917, no one knew exactly what his future held. But one thing was certain: As a member of the **boisterous** and large Kennedy clan, he was going to be a success.

The second of Joseph and Rose's nine children, Jack, as he was called, came from an influential and wealthy family that demanded their children keep up the powerful line. Even his name, John Fitzgerald, was a reminder of

his important roots. He was named after his mother's father, John Francis Fitzgerald, a former mayor of Boston who everyone called Honey Fitz because his legendary charm made him appear sweet on the outside.

Born into a rich Boston Irish family, Rose found someone even more ambitious than her father when she married Joe Kennedy. While Jack's mom was neither a warm nor affectionate mother (although her children never doubted she loved them), Joe was a demanding father who expected all his children to perform well academically, athletically, and socially. He wasn't asking them to do anything he hadn't done himself. Joe, one of the richest men in the nation at the time, was a huge success in a wide range of fields from finance to show business to public service.

Joe made a lot of money by investing in stocks and real estate. He was also a Hollywood movie producer and studio owner. When President Franklin D. Roosevelt created the U.S. Securities and Exchange Commission, the government agency in charge of the stock market, he put Joe in command. Eventually, President Roosevelt made him the ambassador to the United Kingdom. Joe was so savvy that he was one of the few **moguls** to get his investments out of the stock market before the crash of 1929 that marked the start of the Great Depression.

The nine Kennedy kids, who never wanted for anything, weren't afraid to enjoy their great privilege. They attended elite private schools, such as Jack's high school, Choate, and vacationed in one of their many grand homes. Whether on the waters around Cape Cod or Palm Beach, they were confident sailors. The boisterous, good-looking, and tight-knit siblings

Hard Times for Everyone But the Kennedys

The Great Depression was a period of time when the entire American economy collapsed and a lot of the country was out of work. Many people in the United States and around the world lost much or all of their money. But not the Kennedys. Joe's fortune was intact during the ten-year depression that coincided with Jack's childhood. About thirty years later, when a journalist asked him what he remembered of the Great Depression, Jack said he only learned about it during one of his courses at Harvard. He did have one memory of his father hiring "some extra gardeners just to give them a job so they could eat."

were always competing with one another and not just during the outdoor sports they loved to play. Jack, his older and two younger brothers, and four of his five younger sisters, vied to see who could be the smartest, wittiest, and most interesting of the group.

Jack's eldest brother, Joe Jr., was the perfect Kennedy child. He was **charismatic**, a great student, and a super sportsman. He was also the favorite of his father, who planned for his oldest son to enter politics from the time he was little. In fact, Joe Sr. often spoke of Joe Jr.

Jack's Special Sister

Rosemary, the oldest of the Kennedy girls, was born severely mentally handicapped. All the other kids, including Jack, included her in as much as they could and treated her as an equal even though she had trouble speaking. Having Rosemary as a sister meant that Jack developed a great deal of compassion for people with special needs.

becoming president one day. Jack looked up to his dad and wanted some of his attention. But Jack didn't receive much notice with his father's namesake around.

Despite Joe Jr.'s golden-boy status, he was very competitive—particularly with Jack. The rivalry between Joe Jr. and Jack was legendary. Joe Jr. once challenged his younger brother to a bicycle race around the block coming from

opposite sides. Neither boy was willing to admit defeat and swerve away, so they met in a terrible crash in front of their house. Joe Jr. was unhurt, but Jack needed twenty-eight stitches.

Even though Jack always seemed to get the short end of the stick, he loved his brother Joe Jr. fiercely. In his constant competition with his older, stronger brother, it didn't help that Jack was often sick as a young boy. His health had been a problem ever since he had come down with scarlet fever as a two-year-old. Jack's father was so scared his young son was going to die of the potentially fatal disease that he went to the hospital every day for a month until Jack got better.

As a kid, Jack had chicken pox, whooping cough, German measles, mumps, and a number of other infections and illnesses!

At fourteen, Jack only weighed 117 pounds and was no match for his much heartier older brother. The subject of his health was something he didn't like to talk about much, but it must have been a source of sorrow. His recurring illnesses made it difficult for him to really achieve excellence in the sports he loved to play—a fact that didn't go unnoticed by his

father. Joe Sr. often remarked cruelly that he thought his son's poor health was a sign of weakness.

Jack's many illnesses also meant that he had to miss a lot of school, which didn't help his grades any (he was only an average student, excelling in classes such as history, English, and math, and barely scraping by in courses like science and Latin). His teachers and his parents—particularly his demanding father—thought he could do better if he would focus more on his studies and less on sports.

Jack the Big Reader

Jack became a big reader as a way to pass all the time he had to spend in bed while sick. He developed a passion for getting lost in a good book and particularly loved adventure stories. These included the tales of King Arthur's court and historical novels by Sir Walter Scott, a popular Scottish writer from the nineteenth century. He even began subscribing to the *New York Times* when he was fifteen, and he read it every day.

Although he wasn't the best student in the world, Jack entered Princeton as a freshman. Although Princeton is one of the best universities in the world, it wasn't Harvard—his father's alma mater and the school his older brother, Joe, attended. Jack's frail health struck again, and he became so sick during his first year at college, he had to return home. When he recovered, he decided to apply to Harvard even though his grades weren't good enough for him

to get in. Through his family's influence, and not his merits, Jack was accepted.

At Harvard, Jack was back in Joe Jr.'s shadow. He still wasn't as good an athlete or student as his older brother, but at college, he carved out a place that was all his own. Charming and an expert at having a good time, Jack made people feel at ease with his casual manner and intent way of listening. Jack's popularity at Harvard was a sign of things to come.

CHAPTER
TWO

Going to War, Growing Up

In the summer of 1937, Jack went on trips through Europe, courtesy of his father. As he traveled through France, Germany, Italy, and England, Jack enjoyed delicious food, beautiful sights, and stimulating company. He also saw firsthand countries that would soon be at war with one another. His summer vacation through Europe, less than two years before Germany invaded Poland and World War II began, sparked a deep interest in foreign affairs. Upon his return to Harvard, Jack studied politics and international affairs, and during his final two years in college he turned into a much better and more serious student.

A little more than a year after his graduation from Harvard in 1940, Jack signed up for the navy just like his brother Joe. Again, the only way he got in was through his family's influence. Jack had ruptured a disk in his spine while playing football in college and never fully recovered. Despite his bad back, the navy accepted him. While Joe was a flyer, sent to Europe, Jack went to sea. After attending officer training school, he was assigned to the Motor Torpedo Boat squadron. Eager to be on the front where the action was, Lieutenant Jack Kennedy requested combat experience. He arrived in the Solomon Islands on April 14, 1943, where he took command of the small, fast *PT-109* patrol torpedo boat.

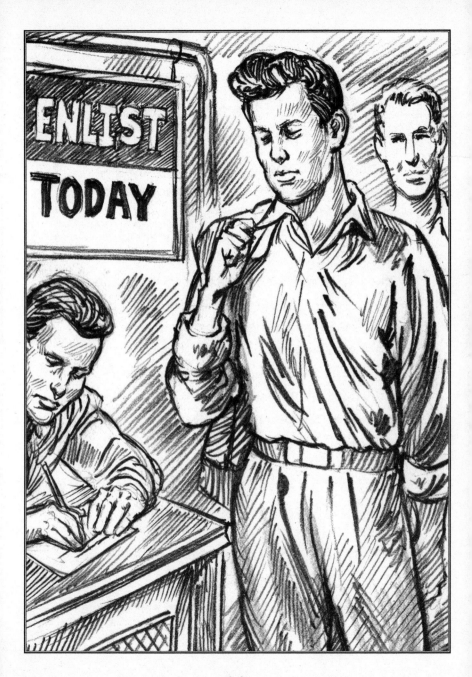

Jack's Bestselling
Senior Thesis

When Jack decided to write his senior thesis about why England's leaders hadn't prepared for the possibility of World War II, he had a very good source of information: his father! Joe Sr., who had been appointed ambassador to the United Kingdom in January 1938, and was living in London, supported his son's long essay on the subject by paying for him to return to Europe in the summer of 1938 and introducing him—as the ambassador's son—to the powerful elite at home and abroad. It was the kind of research that most students could only dream of, and Jack took full advantage of it. His thesis was so good, he turned it into a short book, *Why England Slept*, which received positive reviews and became a bestseller in the United States and Britain.

Jack, who had spent a lot of his life sailing with his family, was comfortable on the water. Even though he was rich and sickly, two traits that might have made him unpopular with his crew, he got along well with everyone. The twelve men under his command liked his easygoing ways and respected his patriotism. But the real test of Jack's ability as a leader came on the night of August 2, 1943. That's when his boat, one of fifteen small vessels sent to intercept a convoy of Japanese ships delivering supplies to Kolombangara Island, suddenly found itself with a Japanese destroyer heading for it at full speed. There had been a problem with communications, and Jack's boat had no radar, so he couldn't see the ship coming in the darkness until it was upon them.

Jack tried to steer out of the way of the much bigger Japanese ship, but it was too late. The warship rammed into *PT-109* and split it

in half! Two of his men were killed instantly on impact, and their deaths weighed on him for the rest of his life. Jack was thrown into the cockpit, injuring his already weak back. Despite his injury, Jack organized the rest of the survivors, who, in the darkness and cold seawater, clung to the sinking hull for four hours. At sunrise, he led his men to a tiny island about three miles away.

One of his men, Patrick "Pappy" McMahon, had serious burns on his hands and face from the explosion the boat made on impact. Pappy didn't think he could make the swim and wanted to give up. But Jack wouldn't let him. Jack clenched a strap from Pappy's life jacket between his teeth and dragged the injured man for the entire five-hour swim to shore.

After getting his men settled on the deserted island, Jack swam back into the sea to search for other PT boats—despite heavy currents and the fact that he hadn't slept in thirty-six hours. There were no boats to be found, however, so Jack and another crew member led the group to a larger nearby island in search of people and supplies. All they found was some candy.

After six days on the deserted island with nothing to eat but the salvaged candy and coconuts, two natives of the Solomon Islands discovered the crew and took a message Jack

After Jack and his men were rescued, he got the coconut shell back. He kept it for the rest of his life. After he became president, it sat on his desk in the Oval Office.

scratched on a coconut to the nearest naval base. The next day the crew was rescued.

Jack, who proved heroic under pressure, wrote to his parents that he was proud of the brave men fighting alongside him. Still, the experience of losing two of his men provided him with firsthand knowledge of combat's terrible toll.

Unfortunately, the death of his two crew members would not be Jack's greatest loss. In August 1944, his brother Joe was killed when his aircraft exploded over England. The news

38

came as a terrible shock to the family, which
turned to Jack, now the eldest son, to embody
all its hopes for political power.

As president, Jack established the United
States Navy's Sea, Air, and Land teams,
otherwise known as the Navy SEALs. The
elite special-ops force carries out secret,
high-pressure missions behind enemy
lines.

CHAPTER
THREE

Courting the Country— and Jackie

Jack wasn't so sure he wanted to go into politics, but after Joe Jr.'s death, his dad decided that's what he was going to do—and whatever Joe Sr. wanted, Joe Sr. got. If his eldest son couldn't become president, then his second eldest would.

Jack loved reading and writing about history. And he'd already had one bestseller on the subject. In fact, he said that if his brother had lived, "I'd have kept on being a writer." Instead, he did as his family expected and was launched with full Kennedy force into his first run, in 1946, for a vacant congressional seat in Massachusetts. Jack won, and then after three terms decided to run for the Democratic Senate seat.

The family support for Jack's political campaign was **formidable**. His younger brother

Bobby was Jack's campaign manager at only twenty-seven years old, and his mother, Rose, and his sisters held teas in Jack's honor for the women voters of Massachusetts. Meanwhile, Jack traveled from town to town, sleeping in cheap motels, eating cheeseburgers and drinking milk shakes, shaking the hands of ordinary folks, and articulating his vision for the future. He was surprisingly popular with the working class despite his privileged upbringing. Just as he had with his navy crew members, Jack won people over with his ability to listen to their problems and his energetic promises to bring about change. With both the working class and the wealthy on his side, Jack won the Senate seat.

It was clear Jack had a bright political future, but what about a family of his own? The answer to that question came when he met Jacqueline Lee Bouvier at a dinner party in 1952. Jackie was from a very wealthy family in New York, and she inhabited the same level of society as Jack. In fact, she was a star in her set. Beautiful and graceful, she was named **Debutante** of the Year in 1947. But Jackie wasn't just a pretty face; she was smart, too. She studied at Vassar College, the Sorbonne in Paris, and George Washington University. After graduating from college, she didn't marry right out of school, which was the usual path for women in her circle. Instead, she got a job as a photographer/reporter at the *Washington Times-Herald* newspaper.

Jack had a lot of respect for Jackie's intelligence, and the two had a shared love of reading. So instead of courting her with candy and flowers, Jack sent her books. And these weren't books of love poems, either. One was *The Raven*, a biography of Sam Houston, an important political figure who lived among the Cherokee Indians and helped make Texas part of

45

the United States. Another, *Pilgrim's Way*, was the autobiography of John Buchan, the Scottish historian, politician, and novelist whose most famous book, *The Thirty-Nine Steps*, was made into a movie by Alfred Hitchcock. Jackie must have found something romantic in Jack's efforts, because the two married on September 12, 1953.

With a successful career in politics and a beautiful, smart wife, Jack seemed to have it

Jack and Jackie's Wedding by the Numbers

When Jack, who was by then a U.S. senator, married Jackie, it was *the* social event of the season, if not the year! Here are some of the wedding's staggering stats.

4 feet of wedding cake.

10 bridesmaids.

50 yards of silk taffeta to make Jackie's dress, which was designed by African American designer Ann Lowe.

800 people invited to attend the ceremony at St. Mary's Catholic Church in Rhode Island.

1,200 guests who joined the happy couple at the reception held at Hammersmith Farm, the seaside estate belonging to Jackie's mother and stepfather.

3,000 onlookers waiting outside the church for a glimpse of the bride. At one point, the crowd broke through police lines and almost crushed Jackie.

all. However, his terrible health problems continued to plague him. His brother Bobby said "at least one half of the days that he spent on this earth" were in pain. In 1947, Jack was diagnosed with Addison's disease, which occurs when the adrenal glands don't produce enough hormones.

If Jack hurt all over, his back was the worst. The combination of Addison's with his

Addison's Disease

If Addison's disease—the symptoms of which include weight loss and weakness—goes untreated, the circulatory system can collapse completely. The estimated nine thousand Americans with the disease today combat it with synthetic hormones. But during Jack's time, there was no such treatment. Instead, he took a host of drugs, vitamins, and steroids to deal with the debilitating symptoms.

injuries from football and the war created an excruciating chronic condition that got so bad while he was in the Senate that he underwent back operations in 1954 and 1955, one of which nearly killed him. Each time Jack had a crisis, his family was called to his bedside to witness a Catholic priest deliver last rites.

During his long recuperation from the 1955 back operation, Jack said the only "solution and

50

salvation" to sitting in bed for months was to find an interesting project to focus on. That project was his book *Profiles in Courage*, about eight U.S. senators, who, as Jack explained, "at crucial periods in our country's history took a decision against the wishes of their **constituents**. In some cases, giving up their careers for the national interest." Published in 1956, his book won the Pulitzer Prize for Biography one year later. Not bad for a side project!

CHAPTER
FOUR

Going for the Presidency

It was official: Jack was running for president of the United States. The handsome, dynamic politician felt up to this huge challenge. From the highest office in the country, he hoped to improve lives and shape history the way great leaders had in all the biographies he had read over the years. Jack had more than enough spirit for the job, but what about experience? He was only forty-two years old when he decided to run.

Not only would Jack be the youngest man elected, he would also be the first Roman Catholic president—something many Americans at the time couldn't imagine happening because of their prejudice against the religion.

If he won, he would be the youngest person ever elected to the office.

The official decision came in 1960, but Jack had been prepping for the campaign ever since the 1956 Democratic Convention. There he had delivered the important nomination speech for Adlai Stevenson, the former governor of Illinois who eventually lost to the Republican and well-loved war hero Dwight D. Eisenhower. The conventions that year were only the second to be televised, and with the understanding of the importance of appearing comfortable and in control on TV, Jack practiced by doing broadcasts. Jack's hard work paid off. His speech was so popular that a lot of the delegates got phone calls from their constituents, who liked the looks of the handsome, charismatic young senator.

Just one week before the 1960 convention, Jack got some very bad news for his chances of winning the Democratic nomination. Two new, powerful politicians challenged him by announcing their candidacies. They were Lyndon B. Johnson, the Senate majority leader

The national Republican and Democratic conventions are large gatherings of delegates from every state who vote on which candidate from the party should run for president. These days, the candidate is usually known before the convention. In Kennedy's year, however, there were several contenders, so no one knew until the final roll call of the delegates who would be nominated as the presidential candidate.

from Texas, and Adlai Stevenson, trying for the presidency a second time. No one knew what was going to happen—including Jack. In the end, though, the delegates decided to take a chance on young Jack.

When Jack won, he surprised a lot of people by selecting Lyndon Johnson as his running mate.

A Family Affair

As they did with all his campaigns, the Kennedy clan got behind Jack's run for president. His father was a strategist behind the scenes and provided emotional support when times got tough, while his mother campaigned in key states. Jack's youngest brother, Ted (who would become a U.S. senator), coordinated the Western states, while Bobby ran his overall campaign. His brother-in-law Stephen Smith was his campaign manager at their headquarters in Washington, D.C. Jackie did a huge amount of campaigning for her husband as well. Impressing the Kennedys with her energy and political skill, she once smilingly convinced the manager of a supermarket in Kenosha, Wisconsin, to let her borrow his PA system, which she used to tell the women in the store, "Just keep on with your shopping while I tell you about my husband, John F. Kennedy."

The Texas senator had grown up without all the advantages that Jack had had. After borrowing the seventy-five-dollar entrance fee to enroll in college, Johnson had worked as a janitor and office page to earn money while he was in school. Elected to Congress in 1937 and then the Senate in 1948, Johnson brought much-needed experience to the team.

If Jack had thought Lyndon and Adlai were formidable opponents, the Republican

Communism is a system in which goods and property are jointly owned by all the members of a society. In a Communist country, everyone from the president to a garbage collector is considered equal, and the government provides people with their basic needs. The Soviet Union's government was run by the Communist Party and was in direct opposition to America's system of democracy.

The ongoing hostility between the Soviet Union (and all the countries it controlled) and the United States (and all the countries it dominated) was called the Cold War. The name came from the fact that the two global superpowers both created a huge arsenal of nuclear weapons to use against each other—but neither side ever fired a shot. If they had, it would have resulted in complete annihilation of both countries, and many others besides.

candidate, Richard M. Nixon, was going to be really tough to beat. At the time, Richard was a two-term vice president with a reputation for being really tough with communists in America and overseas. His aggressive position was popular at the time since the United States and the Soviet Union were in the thick of the Cold War to see which way of life (communism or capitalism) would come to dominate the world.

Jack, on the other hand, had only one term in the U.S. Senate under his belt and basically no experience with foreign affairs. It seemed as if Jack would need a miracle to win.

The miracle that saved Jack was television. The first nationally televised presidential debates between Richard M. Nixon and John F. Kennedy attracted about seventy million American viewers. They all tuned in to watch the seasoned politician debate the young upstart. The outcome was astonishing. Jack came off as being much more appealing, confident, and in control than Richard. Some of the reasons for that were purely superficial and coincidental. Because of a knee injury that landed him in the hospital for two weeks that summer, Richard was twenty pounds underweight and his normal skin tone hadn't yet come back. Still, he refused to put on makeup that would have given him a healthier complexion. His clothes didn't help

him much, either. Not only was he wearing a shirt that didn't fit him, but also, his light gray suit blended into the studio's background, which was the same color. On television, it had the effect of making it look as though Richard was a disembodied head. In contrast, Jack looked crisp and vital in a dark blue suit, despite his chronic health problems. The Kennedy-Nixon debates are considered a turning point in American history because they marked the beginning of television's importance in the election process. The debates also turned a dark horse candidate into the front-runner.

The two men, however, were neck and neck right up until the end. On November 8, 1960, Jack and Jackie (who was eight months pregnant with their second child) cast their votes in Boston and then traveled to Cape Cod to wait for the returns to come in. Because it was such a tight race, election night was very tense. By four in the morning, several states were still too close to call. That's when Jack dragged himself away from the returns to get a little sleep. In the morning, his three-year-old daughter, Caroline, woke him by saying, "Good morning, Mr. President."

Jack won the presidential election by only 118,500 votes!

CHAPTER
FIVE

Life in the White House

Jack didn't want to waste any time when it came to starting the business of being president. He told his staff to be at their desks at 9:00 a.m. the day after the inauguration on Friday, January 20, 1961. But when he got to his desk that Saturday morning, he found the bare walls of the Oval Office so irritating he returned to the White House's living quarters to collect some things to liven them up. In addition to photos of his wife and kids, he chose a watercolor painted by Jackie to hang immediately.

Luckily for Jack, his wife had excellent taste, and she set about using it to restore the first family's residence, which had become quite shabby over the years. From unused rooms and the underground warren of basements in the White House, Jackie unearthed items that belonged to the administrations of past presidents such as Thomas Jefferson and James

The *Resolute* Desk

One of the most interesting and important objects Jackie found during her expeditions around the White House was a huge desk beautifully carved out of wood taken from the British warship HMS *Resolute*. The desk, originally a present from Queen Victoria to President Rutherford B. Hayes in 1880, was the one President Franklin D. Roosevelt sat at while he recorded his famous Fireside Chats

radio broadcasts during the Great Depression. It had been used in other rooms after Roosevelt left office and was only brought back to the Oval Office after Jackie discovered it.

Monroe. She then dusted off these national treasures and put them on display around the White House.

Jackie spent a lot of time completely refurbishing the White House—including its library—so that it would be a proud representation of the country's heritage. When at last she was done, she invited a CBS camera crew in to film a personal tour. In the broadcast, which was viewed on February 14, 1962, by fifty-six million viewers, the thirty-one-year-old First Lady showed off many of the highlights

of the restoration of the fifty-four-room, sixteen-bath mansion. These included a piano designed by President Franklin D. Roosevelt, and the dining room where Thomas Jefferson first introduced the foreign foods of macaroni, waffles, and ice cream to the United States.

Jackie's White House tour for CBS won her an honorary Emmy Award!

Jackie, who was concerned with historic preservation well beyond her time as First Lady, requested the passage of a law that anything the White House acquired become part of its permanent collection. The law states that if future first families aren't using an item in the mansion, it must be given to the Smithsonian for proper housing.

The First Lady brought style to all fronts of the White House. She organized a lot of

important events there so that the mansion not only looked beautiful but also served as a cultural center for the nation. But more than her fine taste in art, architecture, music, or literature, Jackie was known for her amazing sense of fashion. The ultimate trendsetter, she was followed by the press and fans like a movie star. Her signature bobbed hairstyle was copied by women all over the world. When the Kennedys traveled to Paris, thousands of people lined the streets to catch a glimpse of the famous couple. The chic Parisians, however, were especially interested in Jackie. Jack even began a speech he gave during the trip by joking, "I am the man who accompanied Jacqueline Kennedy to Paris."

Jackie was one reason the Kennedy White House was so popular at home and abroad, but there were two more reasons: Caroline and John F. Kennedy, Jr. When Jack took office, his daughter was three and his son, nicknamed John-John, was only two months old. Brother and sister brought a lot of energy to a place usually filled with old people. They liked to do kid things like hide under their dad's desk—especially John, who was a big rascal. As a toddler, he liked to sneak under his father's desk during meetings with staff members and then pop out of a secret compartment.

Caroline and John's mother, aware of what a remarkable opportunity her children had growing up in the White House, started a school for Caroline and her friends in the Solarium on the third floor of the mansion. Even though all she had to do to show up for class was come

upstairs, Caroline didn't want to be different from the other students. So she always put on her coat and lined up with her classmates at a special entrance to the White House that the children used.

Because the school's play yard was right outside the president's private study, sometimes during recess Jack would come outside and clap his hands twice, which was a special signal to Caroline that he had a few minutes to spend with her. Even though he was a very busy man, Jack always made time for his children. He especially loved to share one of his favorite activities with them—reading!

The White House Becomes a Zoo

The Kennedys had a lot of pets at the White House. When they moved in, they brought a Welsh terrier named Charlie. Four other dogs followed, including Pushinka, who was a gift from the leader of the Soviet Union, Nikita Khrushchev. There were also guinea pigs, rabbits, and two hamsters that had a habit of escaping from their cages. The most famous Kennedy pet, however, was Caroline's pony, Macaroni. The pony was well loved, although he sometimes got into trouble. Once the president caught Macaroni munching on shrubs in the Rose Garden!

CHAPTER
SIX

Big Troubles

Being president means making a lot of tough decisions—and Jack's presidency was no exception. Almost as soon as he took office, he had to decide whether or not to invade Cuba, a small island nation ninety miles south of Florida.

The trouble with Cuba had begun a few years back when a young, charismatic Communist revolutionary named Fidel Castro overthrew the government. In August 1960, President Eisenhower, who had cut diplomatic ties with Cuba after the revolution, gave $13 million

83

to the Central Intelligence Agency (a non-military agency that uses covert measures to spy on and aid attacks on other countries) to get rid of Castro.

The CIA's plan was to start the invasion at a place in Cuba called the Bay of Pigs. The spy agency made contact with Cuban exiles in Central America, sending equipment and soldiers to train them so that they could invade Cuba and overthrow Castro. As Jack considered the opinions of his military advisors, he worried

about the possibility of communism gaining a foothold so close to the United States with Castro running Cuba as an ally of the Soviet Union.

Jack agreed with his military advisors that invading Cuba and getting rid of Castro was important to the nation's security, since Cuba was so close to the United States. On April 16, 1961, fourteen hundred Cuban soldiers set out for the Bay of Pigs from nearby Nicaragua by boat. The plan relied on the Cuban people to support the U.S. invasion, but that didn't happen. Instead, Castro's forces crushed the invaders in just three days.

The defeat was a major embarrassment for the United States. Although he had only been in office for four months, and the plan hadn't been his to begin with, Jack immediately took the blame for it. He believed in the phrase that Harry Truman kept on a plaque during his presidency: "The buck stops here." That meant that everything that happened during the president's time in office was ultimately his responsibility.

Just six months later, though, Jack faced the ultimate responsibility—the possibility of starting a nuclear war with the Soviet Union that could have destroyed the entire world! The morning of October 16, 1962, was like any

other for Jack. He was eating breakfast and reading the paper when his national security adviser arrived and handed him photographs that showed some alarming news: The Soviet Union was building nuclear missile launch sites in nearby Cuba.

After the president ordered an emergency meeting of his National Security Council, the first thing he did was call his brother Bobby, then attorney general. He told his brother, whose advice he'd relied upon to get elected, to drop everything and come to the White House immediately. After the Bay of Pigs disaster, when he had followed the advice of military advisors he didn't know that well, Jack was determined to do what he thought was best. But he needed his brother by his side.

It was a very tense time in the White House and the rest of the country. Jack said it was "insane" that he and the Soviet Union's leader, Nikita Khrushchev, "should be able to decide to bring an end to civilization." U.S. troops were put on alert on home soil, and an invasion force massed in Florida. Jack had to figure out a way to stand tough without starting a war. It was not going to be easy.

Instead of launching fighter planes to drop bombs on the missile base, which would have instantly meant war, the president set up a naval blockade around Cuba, preventing Soviet ships from getting to Cuba to drop off weapons, personnel, and supplies. No one was sure how Khrushchev would react to the move.

Kids Take Cover

American schoolchildren during the 1950s and '60s were given drills at school in case of a nuclear attack. They were taught to duck under their desks and cover their heads with their arms when the siren sounded. This was called "duck and cover."

Khrushchev, also realizing the terrible destruction war between the two powers would cause, agreed to a deal where the Soviets got rid of the weapon sites. In exchange, the United

States had to promise it wouldn't invade Cuba again and that it would remove its nuclear missiles from an American base in Turkey.

After the Cuban Missile Crisis, as the event became known in history, Jack became a firm believer in the need for international rules around nuclear weapons. There was simply too much at stake. "We all inhabit this small planet," he said in a speech at American University. "We all breathe the same air. We all cherish our children's future. And we are all mortal."

Jack cared deeply about the future of the world and wanted to use his position as president to promote peace. Six weeks after he was inaugurated, he established the Peace Corps, an organization of volunteers who would live and work in other countries as representatives of the United States for two years at a time. By the end of 1964, more than ten thousand Peace Corps

The Limited Nuclear Test Ban Treaty—
which banned tests with nuclear material
underwater, in the atmosphere, and in
space—was signed by the United States,
the Soviet Union, and the United Kingdom
in August 1963. The treaty allowed
nuclear tests to continue in underground
locations.

Volunteers had served in forty-six countries, building and repairing roads, teaching children to read and write, providing basic medical care, and planning long-term projects to improve the lives of the people they were living with. As a tribute to Jack's legacy, the volunteers were known as "Kennedy's kids."

CHAPTER
SEVEN

A President for All the People

The 1960s was a time of great social change. Many people faced discrimination because of their religion, gender, race, or ethnicity and were demanding fair treatment from those in power. Some of the most oppressed people during the 1960s were black Americans.

Legally segregated from whites in many places around the country, especially in southern states, African Americans weren't allowed to go to the same schools, ride in the same sections on busses, or use the same drinking fountains! Separate facilities were not equal—the schools, water fountains, and other things made available to black people were **inferior** to those available to whites.

The civil-rights movement, which fought for equal treatment under the law for everyone, no matter his or her skin color, came to national attention in 1955 after a black woman named Rosa Parks decided to take a stand by sitting. Rosa Parks was a seamstress who was arrested after she refused to give up her seat at the front of a bus in Montgomery, Alabama, so that a white person could sit down instead. After starting a public, yearlong bus boycott, which led to a Supreme Court decision that declared laws requiring segregated buses to be **unconstitutional**, Rosa became an unlikely hero of the movement.

Even though laws were changing, it wasn't happening fast enough for a lot of civil-rights leaders, including a young minister named Martin Luther King, Jr. Television images of black Americans in the South having vicious police dogs set on them or being hosed by water cannons shocked many Americans. Jack believed the treatment of black people in the United States was a horrible injustice. But his commitment to his beliefs was tested often as a politician.

One such moment came in 1960, while he was running for president. After King had been arrested in Atlanta, Georgia, and sentenced to four months' hard labor related to a traffic violation, Jack wanted to call the civil-rights leader's wife, Coretta, to console her. There were concerns in his campaign that just by making that call (the kind of thing white people running

for office didn't do), he would be hurting his popularity with white southern voters. He called her anyway, and even though it was just a phone call, it made him very popular with black voters. During the election, more than 70 percent of African Americans voted for him!

After Jack became president, tensions between those who believed in the civil-rights movement and those fighting against it only grew stronger. Sometimes, Jack even found himself at odds with people working in his own government. That was the case when James Meredith, a young black man and air force veteran, had won the right in court to become the first black student in the University of Mississippi's 113-year history. The governor of Mississippi, however, was dead set against it. Jack and the governor had several phone calls to discuss the issue, but the governor wouldn't budge on his racist decision. Meanwhile, violent

riots were breaking out near campus. Jack believed James had every right to attend the university, but he worried James might be badly injured—or worse, killed. This was unacceptable to Jack. So he used the full force of his position to protect the young man. On October 1, 1962, James attended his first day of classes with five hundred military policemen watching his back.

Jack was committed to civil rights through

his presidency because he believed it was the right thing to do. No advisor could change his mind on this issue, even as he began his campaign for reelection and his stance on equal rights hurt his chances of becoming president again.

CHAPTER
EIGHT

A Life Cut Short

As Jack and Jackie, in her fashionable pink suit and matching trademark pillbox hat, descended from Air Force One at Love Field in Dallas on November 22, 1963, a crowd of supporters greeted them enthusiastically. The president and glamorous First Lady had received the same warm reception at the airports in Fort Worth, San Antonio, and Houston (where Jackie greeted the crowd in Spanish).

They were on a tour of Texas because

the southwestern state was one of the big
battlegrounds in Jack's campaign for the 1964
reelection. Jack very much wanted another term
as president because he had so much more he
hoped to accomplish. A lot of Texans didn't
support the president's position on civil rights,
though, so he was visiting to give them a dose of
his irresistible charm. Jack loved meeting people
and he understood how powerful a symbol he

was—especially with his wife by his side.

The tour had been going great and the visit to Dallas was no exception. Someone had handed Jackie a large bouquet of red roses at the airport, which she took with her into the waiting limousine that was to carry her and the president, as well as Texas governor John Connally and his wife, Nellie, to a lunch where Jack was speaking. Along the ten-mile route downtown, crowds waved excitedly. They were thrilled to get such a good look at the Kennedys, who sat in the backseat of the convertible limo, whose plastic bubble top had been left off since it was no longer raining.

"You certainly can't say that the people of Dallas haven't given you a nice welcome," Nellie turned around in her seat to say to the president.

These were the last words he was to hear.

Shots rang out at 12:30 p.m. in Dealey Plaza. The president was hit twice in the neck and a

third time in the back of the head, after which he fell sideways into his wife's lap. Governor Connally was seriously wounded in the shooting as well, but he recovered.

Clint Hill, a Secret Service agent, jumped into the car, covered the president's body with his own, and placed one hand on Jackie's shoulder to keep her down as well. The car raced to a nearby hospital, but it was too late. Jack was pronounced dead at 1:00 p.m.—right after a Catholic priest administered last rites.

An hour and a half later, his body was back

on Air Force One, where Lyndon Johnson was sworn in as president with Jackie by his side. Jackie was greeted by Jack's brother Bobby when the plane touched down in Washington, D.C., and he stayed by her side for days.

Jack's death shocked the entire world. He was a powerful symbol of hope both at home and abroad. People believed in the young leader, and now he was gone.

There have always been conspiracy theories about Jack's death. Many people don't believe the killer acted alone. However, no evidence to prove any of those theories has surfaced in the fifty years since the assassination.

Dignitaries from all over the world came to Jack's funeral in Washington, D.C. Charles de Gaulle, the president of France, and Nikita

Jack's Killer

Lee Harvey Oswald was accused of firing the shots at the president from his workplace on the sixth floor of the Texas School Book Depository, which overlooked Dealey Plaza. He was arrested less than an hour after the president's assassination, after allegedly murdering a Dallas police officer. The twenty-four-year-old former marine, who defected to the Soviet Union in 1959, had returned to the United States a year earlier. However, he was still a champion of Communist causes and a political activist on behalf of Fidel Castro. Oswald denied killing both the police officer and the president. No one knows if he was telling the truth because two days after his arrest he was killed by nightclub owner Jack Ruby in the garage of a police station while being taken to a court hearing. Lee, who left behind a Russian widow and two young daughters, died in the same hospital as Jack.

Khrushchev's second in command from Russia walked in the funeral procession with Jackie, Bobby, and Ted Kennedy. As the coffin passed Jackie and the children after the church service, three-year-old John Jr. saluted his father.

Despite his brief time in office, Jack remains one of the most popular presidents in United States history, consistently ranking in the top of various national polls. He and his family captured the country's imagination in ways that few presidents since have managed to. He is remembered as a leader on important issues at home, an effective diplomat on the world stage, and a loving father. The tragic way his own life was cut short could not kill the idealism that Jack inspired in almost everyone. That lives on forever.

10 Things

You Should Know
About John F. Kennedy

1   John "Jack" Fitzgerald Kennedy, born May 29, 1917, was one of nine siblings.

2   As a child, he suffered from many illnesses and was later diagnosed with Addison's disease.

3   He attended Harvard University, but he was only admitted to the school because of family connections.

4
He was awarded the Purple Heart for saving the lives of many of his crew members after a boat collision under his command during World War II.

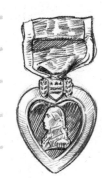

5
Jack served as a member of Congress and as a U.S. senator before he ran for president.

6
He married Jacqueline Bouvier and had two children, Caroline and John. (Jack and Jackie also had a daughter who died at birth, Arabella, and a son who died when he was only two days old, Patrick.)

7 Jack was the youngest person ever elected when he won the presidency on November 8, 1960.

8 Communism was considered one of the biggest threats to the United States while Jack was president.

9 Jack, a firm believer in civil rights, helped get Martin Luther King, Jr., out of jail when he was arrested in Atlanta in 1960. Jack also met with him on the day King delivered his famous "I Have a Dream" speech.

10 Jack was assassinated in Dallas, Texas, on November 22, 1963.

10 MORE Things

That Are Pretty Cool to Know

1 Jack's mom, Rose, kept notecards on each of her nine children, on which she wrote down all the details of their lives from their shoe size to information from a doctor's visit.

2 Even though he was a sickly kid, Jack loved sports and played tennis, basketball, football, and golf during high school.

3 The plane Jack used on the campaign trail was named the *Caroline*, after his daughter.

4 Jack, who sat in a rocking chair a lot to relieve his back pain, helped make it a popular piece of furniture in the United States at that time.

5 During his presidency, Jack made the goal of "landing a man on the moon and returning him safely to the earth." Although this feat was not achieved until 1969, when the astronaut Neil Armstrong was the first person to walk on the moon, it was in large part thanks to Jack's commitment to space exploration.

6 Jack read six newspapers every day while he ate breakfast.

7 The Kennedys made the White House a center of American cultural life by inviting guests such as the famous cellist Pablo Casals, composers Irving Berlin and Leonard Bernstein, and aviator Charles Lindbergh, the first man to fly across the Atlantic Ocean, to visit. Jack's daughter, Caroline, invited cousins and friends over to see films in the White House movie theater.

8 The room that is now used as the press room in the White House has a swimming pool under the floorboards. Jack swam in the pool every day at noon and before dinner. It was heated to 90 degrees because it helped his back pain.

9 Jack was sometimes in such bad physical pain that he couldn't walk without crutches.

10 When Jack ratified the Limited Nuclear Test Ban Treaty into law on October 7, 1963, he used a different fountain pen for each letter of his full name so that they could be given as gifts to the people present at the signing. There were twenty-one pens in all!

Glossary

Boisterous: behaving in a wild and noisy way

Charismatic: someone who is powerfully appealing to other people

Constituents: voters represented by an elected official

Debutante: a young woman from an upper-class family

Dignitary: someone who has a position of honor or respect

Formidable: frightening and awesome

Idealistic: believing that ideals are more important than practical matters

Inferior: not as good; lower in quality

Moguls: prominent people in a particular industry

Tyranny: ruling other people in a cruel or unjust way

Unconstitutional: not in keeping with the basic principles or laws set forth in the Constitution of the United States

Places to Visit

Find your own inspiration from Jack by visiting places from his life, either online or in real life.

John Fitzgerald Kennedy National Historic Site, Brookline, Massachusetts
See Jack's birthplace as it was in 1917! Jack's mother, Rose, commemorated her son after the family repurchased the nine-room house at 83 Beals Street in 1966, by turning it into a museum with original furniture, photographs, and personal objects.
nps.gov/nr/travel/presidents/john_f_kennedy_ birthplace.html

John F. Kennedy Presidential Library and Museum, Boston, Massachusetts
With exhibits on the 1960 Democratic Convention, Kennedy-Nixon debates, Oval Office, and more, visitors to the museum can learn about Jack's life and times. The library's holdings go way beyond Jack's papers to include those of many Kennedy family members as well as the most comprehensive

Ernest Hemingway archive in the world!
jfklibrary.org
virtual museum tour: **whd.jfklfoundation.org/tour**

Jacqueline Kennedy: The White House Tour
*Watch the First Lady give a tour of the beautifully
restored White House as it aired on CBS in 1962.*
hulu.com/watch/5135

The Sixth Floor Museum at Dealey Plaza,
Dallas, Texas
*Visit this museum located in the former Texas
School Book Depository where Lee Harvey Oswald
fired his rifle and assassinated the president.*
jfk.org

President John Fitzgerald Kennedy Gravesite,
Arlington National Cemetery, Virginia
*Jack is buried in the military cemetery, where more
than 400,000 active-duty service members, veterans,
and family members have been laid to rest.*
**http://www.arlingtoncemetery.mil/
VisitorInformation/MonumentMemorials/JFK.aspx**

Bibliography

An Unfinished Life: John F. Kennedy, 1917–1963, Robert Dallek, Back Bay Books, 2004.

DK Biography: John F. Kennedy, Howard S. Kaplan, DK Publishing, 2004.

John F. Kennedy: His Life and Legacy, Shelley Sommer, HarperCollins, 2005.

John F. Kennedy: The Making of a Leader (Time for Kids Biographies), Editors of Time for Kids and Ritu Upadhyay, Perfection Learning, 2005.

John F. Kennedy: Thirty-Fifth President 1961–1963 (Getting to Know the U.S. Presidents), Mike Venezia, Children's Press, 2007.

Sterling Biographies: John F. Kennedy: Voice of Hope, Marie Hodge, Sterling, 2007.

Who Was John F. Kennedy?, Yona Zeldis McDonough, Grosset & Dunlap, 2004.

Index

Also Available

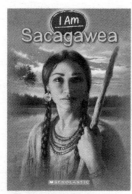

I Am
Sacagawea

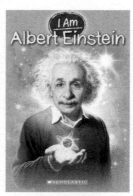

I Am
Albert Einstein

I Am
Helen Keller

I Am
Martin Luther King, Jr.

I Am
George Washington

I Am
Harriet Tubman

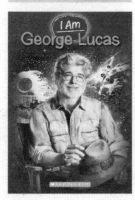

I Am
George Lucas

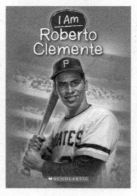

I Am
Roberto Clemente

I Am
John F. Kennedy